SPEAKPRENEUR
TRANSFORM YOUR VOICE TO IMPACT, INFLUENCE & INCOME

PAUL L. GETTER

© 2024 Paul L. Getter

All rights reserved. No part of this publication may be reproduced, distributed, or transmitted in any form or by any means, including photocopying, recording, or other electronic or mechanical methods, without the prior written permission of the publisher, except in the case of brief quotations embodied in critical reviews and certain other noncommercial uses permitted by copyright law. For permission requests, write to the publisher, addressed "Attention: Permissions Coordinator," at the address below.

ISBN: 979-8-218-45947-5

This is a work of nonfiction. While all attempts have been made to verify information provided in this publication, the author does not assume any responsibility for errors, omissions, or contrary interpretation of the subject matter herein. This publication is not intended for use as a source of legal, business, accounting, or financial advice. The reader should consult a professional in any matter relating to his/her business. Any perceived slight of any individual or organization is purely unintentional.

Printed in the United States of America

First Edition

www.Speakpreneur.com

CONTENTS

About The Author — 1

Introduction — 3

1. The Day I Borrowed Lincoln's Beard and Found My Superpower — 5

2. Scoring for the Wrong Team and Other Public Speaking Tips — 15

3. Monsters, Mistakes, and Microphones: A Journey to Fearlessness — 31

4. Father Knows Best: How My Dad Helped Me Find My Voice — 41

5. Bikers, Bowties, and Bridges: The Magic of a Well-Told Speech — 59

6. The Bird Trick That Backfired: A Storytelling Lesson — 73

7. From Broke to Booked: Public Speaking, My   87
   Passport to Success
8. The Secret Sauce People Don't Like To Talk   99
   About

My Concluding Thoughts   110

ABOUT THE AUTHOR

Paul Getter is a renowned digital marketer and motivational speaker with a remarkable career. Known as "The Internet Marketing Nerd," Paul has shared his insights on stages worldwide alongside some of the biggest names in the industry, earning substantial success through his high-impact engagements. He has captivated audiences ranging from intimate groups of 50 to massive crowds of 50,000, delivering powerful and transformative messages. His engaging and informative talks have empowered countless entrepreneurs to maximize their online presence, boost their business growth, and achieve their personal and professional goals. With his expertise and dynamic speaking style, Paul has become a sought-after figure in the realms of digital marketing and motivational speaking, inspiring audiences and driving transformative results across the globe.

INTRODUCTION

Hello, future Speakpreneur!

Embarking on this journey to enhance your public speaking skills means unlocking a world of limitless potential. The Speakpreneur path is not just about mastering the art of speaking; it's about finding and harnessing your unique voice to inspire, influence, and leave a lasting impact on those around you.

Throughout these pages, you'll uncover the secrets to captivating audiences, transforming nervousness into confidence, and turning every speech into a powerful catalyst for change. Whether you're addressing a small group or a massive crowd, the principles and techniques in this book will help you become a more compelling and effective communicator.

You'll explore personal stories, engage in practical exercises, and discover proven strategies that will help you connect deeply with your audience, build a robust personal brand, and turn your speaking skills into a lucrative career. From crafting memorable stories to perfecting your delivery, every chapter is designed to empower you to speak with both authority and authenticity.

The journey of a Speakpreneur is not only enriching and fulfilling but also offers the potential for a thrilling and profitable career. Picture yourself traveling the globe, meeting influential individuals, and earning more in a single hour than you once thought possible in a year. Public speaking can open doors to extraordinary opportunities, allowing you to transform your passion into a thriving profession.

So, let's start this exciting and rewarding journey together. Let your voice be heard, your message resonate, and your influence grow. Welcome to the world of Speakpreneurship, where your words can shape the future and your voice can truly change the world.

Let's get started.

CHAPTER ONE

THE DAY I BORROWED LINCOLN'S BEARD AND FOUND MY SUPERPOWER

In the sea of towering figures that filled my school, I was an island of quiet—the shortest, skinniest, and most withdrawn kid in my class. Yet, at the tender age of eight, I stumbled upon what I would come to call my superpower. This discovery was thanks to an unexpected challenge from Mr. Archer, my fourth-grade teacher, known for his unconventional teaching methods. He proposed a quest that seemed Herculean at the time: memorize and recite The Gettysburg Address in one week and earn the honor of portraying Abraham Lincoln in the school play.

Fueled by a mix of naivety and determination, I embraced the challenge. "Four score and seven years ago..." The words of Lincoln became my mantra, echoing through my mind until they were etched into my memory. Surprisingly, I was the lone voyager who dared to navigate this challenge.

I remember the moment vividly: a diminutive, timid eight-year-old stepping onto the stage, the weight of the iconic black top hat pressing down, a makeshift beard awkwardly affixed to my face. The cafeteria was transformed into a sea of expectant faces, a blend of students and parents. My heart pounded as I adjusted the microphone, the bright lights casting long shadows behind me.

Was I nervous? Tremendously. Yet, beneath the surface, a quiet confidence hummed, born from the countless hours I had spent rehearsing. As I uttered the opening phrase, "Four score and seven years ago our fathers brought forth on this continent, a new nation conceived in Liberty..." each word rang out clear and true. I was no longer just a boy; I was a vessel for Lincoln's enduring words.

The applause that followed was thunderous, a standing ovation that seemed to shake the very foundations of the cafeteria. As I took my bow, a realization washed over me: I had not only discovered my voice but had also captivated an audience with the power of spoken word. "Wow!

That was pretty cool. I did a good job." At that moment, I knew I had unearthed my superpower:

The ability to speak in front of people, hold their attention, and confidently convey a message.

This newfound ability became a beacon that guided me through my teenage years, a period marked by social awkwardness and shyness. Yet, paradoxically, when faced with a crowd, I found solace. Speaking to an audience, no matter its size, felt as natural as breathing, a stark contrast to my stuttering conversations in one-on-one interactions.

My peers often questioned this anomaly, curious why the specter of public speaking, which haunted so many, seemed to bypass me entirely. I didn't have a clear answer for them. Perhaps it was because no one had ever told me to be afraid of speaking in public. Or maybe, in the act of speaking, I found a connection to others that eluded me in everyday interactions.

This journey from a shy, unassuming child to a confident speaker taught me an invaluable lesson: within each of us lies a superpower waiting to be discovered. For me, it was the ability to stand before a crowd and share a message, a skill that has shaped my life in ways I could never have imagined.

In my journey, I've come to realize that public speaking is not just a skill; it's a key that unlocks doors to worlds I never dreamed possible. This art has been my passport, allowing me to traverse the globe, from the echoing halls of prestigious universities to the serene landscapes of distant lands. It has enabled me to witness breathtaking sights—the kind of places you'd only expect to see in glossy travel magazines or as backdrops in epic movie scenes. Through the power of speech, I've had the privilege to touch the hearts and minds of countless individuals, leaving imprints that transcend geographical and cultural boundaries.

But perhaps the most unexpected gift of all has been the financial rewards. Public speaking has proven to be an invaluable asset, one that has significantly elevated my earning potential. It's a stark contrast to the humble beginnings of my youth, where the constraints of poverty seemed like insurmountable walls. The young boy who once faced the world with hesitance and shyness now stands before crowds, sharing insights and inspirations, all the while forging a path of prosperity I once thought was reserved for others.

This revelation brings me to a compelling conclusion: the art of public speaking is an essential tool for everyone, regardless of their field or profession. In today's interconnected world, the ability to communicate effectively and persuasively is a cornerstone of success. Whether you're a budding entrepreneur pitching your next big idea, a dedicated educator inspiring young minds, or a passionate activist advocating for change, the power to convey your message clearly and compellingly can be the difference between being heard and being overlooked.

Investing in public speaking skills is more than just improving your ability to deliver a speech; it's about enhancing your capacity to influence, motivate, and connect profoundly with others. It's about building confidence and credibility, two attributes that can elevate your professional image and open doors to opportunities you never imagined. In essence, learning to master public speaking is an investment in your personal and professional growth, one that can yield dividends in every aspect of your life.

So, I urge everyone, regardless of their background or aspirations, to embrace the journey of becoming an effective public speaker. The benefits extend far beyond the podium; they infiltrate every interaction and every opportunity, transforming how you navigate the world. Embrace this skill and watch as new horizons of possibility unfold before you, painting your future with strokes of success, fulfillment, and unimaginable adventure.

The art of public speaking is an indispensable tool in the entrepreneur's arsenal. It is the bridge between vision and reality, ideas and action. As you venture through the pages of this book, you will uncover the secrets to not only capturing an audience but captivating their hearts and minds. Once unleashed, you will learn that your voice can echo across industries, inspiring innovation and driving progress.

As entrepreneurs, we are not just builders of businesses; we are leaders, influencers, and architects of the future. Speaking is our most potent instrument in this endeavor. It allows us to lead with conviction, influence with integrity, and generate income through impact. Each topic we explore will further equip you with the strategies, insights, and courage needed to step onto any stage—or into any meeting room—and speak with authority and authenticity.

Let this chapter be the foundation upon which you build your Speakpreneur journey. The skills you develop here will not only amplify your message but will also elevate your leadership, enhancing your ability to motivate teams, persuade stakeholders, and engage with your community on a deeper level. Remember, the path to becoming a transformative leader through speaking is a journey of continuous growth and learning. Embrace each opportunity to speak as a way to refine your craft and extend your influence.

As you turn the pages of this book, keep in mind that every word spoken is a seed planted in the garden of possibility. With dedication, practice, and a commitment to excellence, you will watch these seeds grow into towering trees of influence, impact, and income. Welcome to the world of Speakpreneurship, where your voice is your greatest asset, and your message has the power to change the world. Let's embark on this journey together, transforming every whisper of potential into a resounding symphony of success.

EXERCISES:

To help you harness the power of public speaking and uncover your own superpower, try these practical exercises inspired by the themes of this chapter:

1. **Revisit a Challenge**: Think back to a moment in your life when you faced a significant challenge and overcame it. Write down the details of the experience, focusing on what motivated you to take on the challenge and how you felt when you succeeded. Reflect on how this experience can inspire your public speaking.

2. **Memorize and Recite**: Choose a short, powerful speech or passage to memorize. Practice reciting it daily, focusing on your tone, pace, and expression. This exercise will help you build confidence and improve your memorization skills, much like my experience with The Gettysburg Address.

3. **Create a Signature Story**: Develop a personal story that encapsulates your journey or a pivotal moment in your life. Practice telling this story in a way that is engaging and relatable. Your personal story will become your signature story

that you can use to connect with your audience and illustrate your points.

4. **Audience Empathy Exercise**: Imagine you are preparing to speak to an audience that is entirely on your side and wants to see you succeed. Write a short speech or presentation with this supportive audience in mind. Focus on conveying your message with confidence and authenticity, knowing that your audience is there to support you.

5. **Visualization Technique**: Spend a few minutes each day visualizing yourself speaking confidently and successfully in front of an audience. Imagine the positive reactions and feedback from your listeners. Visualization can boost your confidence and reduce anxiety.

6. **Feedback Loop**: Record yourself giving a speech or presentation. Watch the recording and take notes on your performance. Pay attention to your body language, eye contact, and vocal delivery. Identify areas where you can improve and practice those specific aspects. Seek feedback from trusted friends or family members.

7. **Small Speaking Opportunities**: Seek small opportunities to speak in front of others, such as team meetings, family gatherings, or community events. These experiences will help you become more comfortable speaking in front of an audience and provide valuable practice.

> By consistently practicing these exercises, you will build your confidence and develop the skills needed to become an effective and impactful public speaker. Remember, the journey to mastering public speaking is a gradual process, but with dedication and effort, you can achieve your goals.

Chapter Two
Scoring for the Wrong Team and Other Public Speaking Tips

In this chapter, we will unpack an exciting idea: while some skills rely heavily on what you were born with, like height for basketball or brute strength for powerlifting, speaking to a crowd isn't one of those. You might think that being a great speaker is something you're either born with or you're not, but that's not the case. Public speaking is a skill you can build over time, not something you're just stuck with.

Consider basketball players; being tall can give you a huge advantage. And for powerlifting, being naturally big and strong is a big plus. But when it comes to speaking in front of people, your height or how much you can bench press doesn't really matter. What matters is your willingness to practice, learn from feedback, and keep trying even when it gets tough.

This chapter shows you that you don't need to be a specific "type" of person to be good at public speaking. It doesn't matter if you're not the life of the party or if you've always been more of a listener than a talker. Speaking effectively in front of others is about learning the right techniques, practicing them, and not being afraid to make mistakes and learn from them.

We will dive into how anyone can learn to speak confidently and clearly, regardless of their background or natural abilities. Public speaking is about expressing your ideas in a way that connects with others, and with some effort and guidance, anyone can learn to do it well.

Consider my own journey into the world of basketball, influenced by my father's passion for coaching the game. As a child, it was almost predestined that I would lace up my sneakers and take to the court. But was I destined to excel? The answer to that question became amusingly clear during one of my early experiences on the basketball court.

At the age of twelve, I was hardly the picture of athletic promise—more a collection of limbs than a coordinated athlete, with a stature that was more 'short and scrawny' than 'tall and imposing.' Yet, I made up for what I lacked in coordination with enthusiasm and a peculiar advantage: my unusually long arms, which proved surprisingly effective at intercepting passes between unsuspecting opponents.

During one memorable game, a stroke of luck—or perhaps destiny—saw me stealing the ball from the clutches of the opposing team. With the zeal of a seasoned athlete, I sprinted towards the basket, the ball in my hands and the court open before me. The crowd's cheers fueled my determination, their cries of "Go, Go, Go!" a symphony to my ears. With not a single defender in sight, victory seemed assured, the basket an open invitation to glory.

With a heart-pounding in triumph, I executed what felt like a textbook layup. The ball sailed through the air and swished through the net—a flawless score. Or so I thought, until I turned, beaming with pride, ready to bask in the admiration of my teammates. Instead, I was met with a sea of hands clasped overheads, expressions of disbelief painting their faces. It was only after scoring that I realized the truth. The crowd's cries were not of encouragement but of desperate warning. "No, No, No!" they had shouted, not "Go, Go, Go!" In my eagerness, I scored a basket for the opposing team!

As I watched my dreams of becoming a professional basketball player dissolve before my eyes, I couldn't help but confront the harsh truth. My athletic prowess, or rather the lack thereof, along with my stature and innate coordination, starkly underscored my disadvantage in the competitive world of sports. The realization was bitter, marking the end of one dream but, unbeknownst to me, the beginning of another, far more accessible journey.

In the realm of public speaking, I hold a steadfast belief that the doors are wide open for anyone eager to walk through. Unlike the rigid prerequisites of professional sports, the art of oratory does not demand exceptional athleticism or physical superiority. Instead, it extends an invitation to all, promising that anyone can emerge as a compelling speaker with the right guidance, unwavering practice, and dedication to mastering the craft. Shyness, that seemingly impenetrable barrier, can indeed be dismantled. The claws of fear, which clutch at our throats, can be pried loose. The potential to become a powerful communicator resides within each of us.

Indeed, some individuals are graced with natural eloquence, a gift that effortlessly captivates and commands attention. However, the true distinction between a mediocre speaker and one who leaves an indelible mark on their audience is not merely innate talent. It is, rather, a relentless pursuit of excellence, a burning desire to refine and enhance one's skills continually.

I surmise that it is this very passion that has led you to this book. A yearning not just to speak but to speak with purpose, to transform your voice into a tool that can inspire, persuade, and make a lasting impact. You're here because you understand that your voice has the power to change minds, to move hearts, and to shape the future. So, let's embark on this journey together, with a commitment to unlocking that power, and transforming the dream of becoming an influential speaker into reality.

At an event not too long ago, I had the opportunity to reconnect with Carlos, a friend whose outgoing nature and articulate manner had always stood out. Carlos was the kind of person you'd remember for his friendliness and engaging conversations. However, on this particular occasion, when he was suddenly asked to express his thoughts in front of a camera, an unexpected transformation occurred. The Carlos I knew, always brimming with confidence and charm, seemed to vanish, leaving in his place someone who was visibly unnerved. He stuttered, struggled to find his words, and appeared utterly lost. It was a side of Carlos I had never seen before;

he looked like a deer caught in the glare of oncoming headlights, frozen and unsure.

Moved by curiosity and a desire to help a friend, I pulled Carlos aside to a quieter spot. "What's happening?" I asked, hoping to understand his sudden shift. His reply was simple yet filled with vulnerability: "I've never done this before." At that moment, I realized that Carlos, despite his usual confidence, had stumbled upon an unfamiliar challenge. Recognizing an opportunity to assist, I guided him through a brief, focused exercise, aiming to reignite his innate confidence.

The transformation was immediate and remarkable. Carlos shed his apprehension like an old coat, stepping into a newfound confidence with a sparkle in his eye and an eager posture. When he spoke again, his words flowed not just with clarity but with an infectious enthusiasm. The change was profound, not merely in his demeanor but in his entire presence. Carlos had rediscovered his voice, stepping boldly into his potential as a communicator.

This experience proved to be a turning point for Carlos. The next day, he eagerly volunteered to speak in front of a class, embracing the opportunity to tear down the walls of doubt that had momentarily caged his ability to speak publicly. In that classroom, Carlos didn't just talk; he inspired, marking the beginning of his journey as a compelling communicator.

You may wonder what advice I shared with Carlos during that transformative exercise. I'll share more about that later.

But let me leave you with these three powerful tips that every speaker or aspiring speaker must understand:

1. KNOW YOUR AUDIENCE AND SUBJECT INSIDE OUT

Understanding who you are speaking to is crucial. Tailor your message to resonate with your audience's interests, needs, and level of understanding. Similarly, having a deep knowledge of your subject matter boosts your confidence and allows you to speak more persuasively. Research thoroughly, anticipate questions, and prepare to engage your audience with relevant and insightful content. I've spoken in front of 10 people in a small room, and I've also spoken in front of 50,000 people filling a stadium. Each experience is unique and must be treated accordingly.

2. PRACTICE AND REHEARSE

The importance of practice cannot be overstated. Rehearse your speech multiple times, focusing not just on what you're going to say but how you're going to say it. Pay attention to your pacing, intonation, and pauses, which can all dramatically affect the impact of your words. Consider practicing in front of a mirror, recording yourself, or rehearsing in front of a trusted friend or mentor who can provide constructive feedback.

3. MASTER THE ART OF STORYTELLING

Stories have the power to captivate and connect with audiences on a personal level. Incorporate relevant stories, anecdotes, or personal experiences into your speeches to make your message more memorable and engaging. A well-told story can illustrate complex ideas in a relatable way, evoke emotions, and leave a lasting impression on your audience.

Remember, great speakers are not born; they are made through dedication, practice, and a willingness to learn and grow. Embrace feedback, stay authentic to who you are, and let your passion for the subject shine through. With these tips and a commitment to continuous improvement, you'll be well on your way to becoming a compelling and impactful speaker.

Cultivating the habit of maintaining a notebook within easy reach—be it in your car, at your workspace, or any place where you spend considerable time—is invaluable for any aspiring speaker. This practice serves as a reservoir for capturing the fleeting moments of inspiration and the rich tapestry of personal experiences that life unfurls day by day. Encourage yourself to jot down anecdotes, reflections, and narratives as they unfold or as they flutter into your mind. Compile these stories diligently, creating a vibrant mosaic of experiences that uniquely belong to you.

Beyond merely cataloging these tales, dedicate time to ponder how each story can be seamlessly integrated into your speeches. This exercise is not just about stockpiling content; it's about curating a versatile arsenal of illustrations that can breathe life into your presentations, making them resonate more deeply with your audience.

Be perpetually on the lookout for moments that can serve as illustrations or metaphors within your speeches. Every interaction, observation, and personal achievement holds the potential to be transformed into a compelling narrative thread that can enhance your message, making it more relatable and impactful. This ongoing quest for stories encourages mindfulness and creativity, ensuring you're always equipped with fresh, engaging material to weave into your discourse.

This strategy not only enriches your speeches but also sharpens your storytelling skills, enabling you to connect more profoundly with your audience through shared human experiences. Remember, the most memorable speeches are those that weave the personal with the universal, turning individual stories into shared journeys. By cultivating this habit, you're not just collecting stories; you're building bridges of empathy and understanding that can transform your public speaking into a powerful tool for connection and influence.

In closing, it's imperative to embrace the truth that success in public speaking is accessible to anyone willing to invest in the journey. Hard work, unwavering commitment, and steadfast dedication are the cornerstones upon which the foundation of a successful speaker is built. The path may be challenging, strewn with obstacles and moments of self-doubt, but it is also marked by growth, discovery, and the unparalleled satisfaction of finding your voice and making it heard. Remember, the art of speaking is not reserved for a select few; it is a craft that can be mastered by anyone with the courage to start and the perseverance to continue. As we conclude this chapter, carry forward the belief that with determination and effort, you, too, can carve out your place among the voices that inspire, influence, and ignite change.

Go... go... go! You can do it!

EXERCISES:

To help you build your public speaking skills and realize that anyone can be a speaker, try these practical exercises inspired by the themes of this chapter:

1. **Self-Assessment of Speaking Abilities**: Reflect on your current speaking abilities. Write down your strengths and areas for improvement. Identify specific skills you want to develop, such as clarity, pace, or body language. This self-awareness will guide your practice.

2. **Role Reversal Exercise**: Watch a video of a public speaker you admire and then try to deliver a short speech in their style. Focus on mimicking their tone, pacing, and gestures. This exercise helps you experiment with different styles and find what works best for you.

3. **Story Swap**: Partner with a friend or family member and exchange personal stories that you can each use in a speech. Practice telling each other's stories, focusing on making them engaging

and relatable. Story-swapping will enhance your storytelling skills and provide new speech material.

4. **Mindfulness and Relaxation Techniques**: Before you practice speaking, spend a few minutes doing mindfulness exercises or deep breathing to calm your nerves. This will help you enter a state of relaxed focus, which is beneficial for public speaking.

5. **Peer Review**: Form a small group of peers or colleagues who are also interested in improving their public speaking skills. Take turns delivering speeches and providing each other with constructive feedback. This supportive environment will help you grow and learn from others.

6. **Experiment with Different Audiences**: Practice giving the same speech to different types of audiences, such as children, professionals, or friends. Notice how you adapt your language, tone, and examples to suit each group. Different audiences will improve your versatility as a speaker.

7. **Create a Speaking Schedule**: Set a regular schedule for practicing your speeches. Whether it's once a week or every day, consistency is key. Having a dedicated time for practice will help you steadily improve your skills.

By consistently practicing these exercises, you will build your confidence and develop the skills needed to become an effective and impactful public speaker. Remember, the journey to mastering public speaking is a gradual process, but with dedication and effort, you can achieve your goals.

HEY SPEAKPRENEUR!

I HOPE YOU ARE ENJOYING THIS BOOK AND FINDING IT VALUABLE. IF YOU'RE SERIOUS ABOUT TAKING YOUR SPEAKING SKILLS TO THE NEXT LEVEL, I HAVE SOMETHING INCREDIBLY EXCITING FOR YOU.

RIGHT NOW, AT SPEAKPRENEUR.COM, THERE'S AN EXCLUSIVE OPPORTUNITY WAITING JUST FOR YOU. THIS SPECIAL OFFER IS DESIGNED TO HELP YOU ELEVATE YOUR SPEAKING GAME, BUILD A POWERFUL PERSONAL BRAND, AND TURN YOUR TALENT INTO A LUCRATIVE AND EXCITING CAREER. BUT HURRY—THIS OFFER WON'T LAST FOREVER!

DON'T MISS OUT ON THE CHANCE TO TRANSFORM YOUR JOURNEY AND ACHIEVE THE SUCCESS YOU'VE ALWAYS DREAMED OF. VISIT SPEAKPRENEUR.COM NOW AND SEE WHAT AMAZING RESOURCES AND OPPORTUNITIES ARE WAITING FOR YOU. YOUR FUTURE AS A TOP-TIER SPEAKER STARTS HERE!

GO TO SPEAKPRENEUR.COM NOW!

Chapter Three

MONSTERS, MISTAKES, AND MICROPHONES: A JOURNEY TO FEARLESSNESS

As a child, the shadows of the night held a particular terror for me, with every creak and whisper magnified into a chorus of unseen threats. One evening, as I began to drift off to sleep, a peculiar noise jolted me awake. Dismissing it initially with a sleepy shrug, I drifted back towards slumber. Yet, the silence was soon shattered by a more distinct, louder growl—a sound that seemed to crawl straight out of a nightmare. Could it be an intruder, or worse, a monster lurking beneath my bed, waiting in the darkness?

Heart pounding, I sat upright, scanning the shadow-drenched room. My eyes, wide with fear, darted towards the doorway, where a towering figure loomed, its silhouette a dark blot against the faint night light. "Who could it be?" I wondered, terror gripping me. "What did they want?"

In a whisper tinged with dread, I called out to my big brother, my voice barely above a breath, "Bub, Bub...someone's broken into the house...they're at the door." Stirring from his sleep, my brother sensed my panic, only to chuckle, rise, and flick on the light.

The ominous figure that had filled the doorway with menace? Merely my brother's jacket, innocently draped over the door. My embarrassment bloomed as I stammered about the fearsome growling that had awakened me. With a laugh, my brother revealed the source of the growling terror: "Yeah, I hear it every night when you fall asleep... you snore pretty loud."

Thus, the beastly growls that had haunted the night were none other than the sounds of my own snoring. The menacing intruder, poised in the doorway, was nothing more than a coat hanging quietly in its place.

What if the fear of speaking doesn't really exist? What if it's a lie we've told ourselves so many times that we now believe it? Just like my childhood fears, have we convinced ourselves that something terrifying is there when it really isn't?

We've all heard the infamous quote that people fear public speaking more than dying. This often-cited statistic, originating from a 1973 Bruskin Associates survey, claimed that 41% of people feared public speaking more than death. Can I be honest with you? I have never met anyone who, given the choice between public speaking and dying, would choose death!

This one anecdote has discouraged more people from stepping up to the podium than anything else, creating a false narrative that we should instinctively fear speaking in front of an audience.

However, a more recent study by The Chapman University of American Fears in 2015 found that people are more afraid of reptiles, robots, and running out of money than public speaking, with only 28.4% of people reporting a fear of public speaking.

Look, I don't want to downplay the fact that many people feel anxious, nervous, and uncomfortable speaking in public. Even seasoned public speakers experience these feelings.

I recall one of the most significant moments in my public speaking career when I was overwhelmed with fear. My hands trembled, my mouth was dry, and I was sweating nervously. This was in Cali, Colombia, before one of the largest audiences I had ever faced—a stadium filled with over 50,000 people. As I looked out over this vast sea of faces, many thoughts raced through my mind: "Don't mess this up... So many people... ugh!"

But something happened that quickly relieved all my fear, turning it into a learning moment and a tool I use to help others overcome their fear of speaking. Speaking in Colombia was unique because it required a translator. Sammy, a good friend of mine, stood by my side, translating my words in a rhythmic cadence. Noticing my nervousness as we approached the podium, he said, "Paul, the people love you. Don't worry, I gotcha," and chuckled.

That one sentence revealed why I was nervous and why I didn't need to be. It brought me a sense of calmness as I realized a few key things.

First, I understood that the audience was on my side. They were there to support me, not to criticize. These were people who "loved me" and wanted me to succeed.

Secondly, when Sammy said, "Don't worry, I gotcha," I knew exactly what he meant. Having teamed up like this before, he was essentially saying, "Paul, if you mess up, I can fix it when I translate." His chuckle reassured me that I couldn't mess up.

By understanding this, I've learned not only to quiet my own nervousness when speaking publicly but also to help others overcome their fears and anxieties.

How can we apply this?

First, recognize that you are standing in front of your audience because someone believed in you enough to give you the invitation. Most people genuinely want to hear what you have to say.

They are on your side. Yes, there will be critics, but don't focus on them. Recognize that your message, your story, and your experience can help people and even change lives. Let this drive and motivate you. Your words can make a difference; your message can potentially change the world!

Secondly, understand that the fear of making mistakes is natural. Nobody wants to make a big blunder in front of everyone. But most people aren't looking for perfection. Speaking is a skill like any other. The more you practice, the better you will get and the more confident you will become.

Many people say, "Public speaking is hard." The truth is, public speaking is not inherently hard; it just feels challenging because you're currently not good at it. Like any skill, public speaking becomes easier with practice and experience. When you become proficient, what once seemed daunting will feel natural and effortless. Remember, even the best speakers started as beginners. The more time, energy, and practice you invest, the better you will become, and what was once intimidating will become second nature.

Finally, remember that every speaking opportunity is a chance to learn and grow. Embrace feedback, whether positive or constructive. Use it to refine your skills and improve your delivery. The more you speak, the more comfortable and confident you will become. Public speaking is not about being perfect; it's about being genuine, connecting with your audience, and conveying your message effectively.

Remember me telling you about Carlos? What did I say to him that instilled confidence and relieved his fear? I told him a few things: I was by his side and believed he could do it, and the people there liked him—he's a cool guy. I also told him that we could just edit the video if he made a mistake. See what I did there? I reassured him that he wasn't alone, that he was capable, and that mistakes could be fixed. This simple yet profound approach can be applied to your own fears and anxieties about public speaking.

EXERCISES:

To help you conquer your fear of public speaking and build your confidence, try these practical exercises that are directly inspired by the themes of this chapter:

1. **Shadow and Light Exercise**: Just as I realized my fear of the shadows in my room was unfounded, identify an irrational fear related to public speaking. Write it down and then logically break down why it is not as frightening as it seems. Understanding that your fear may be based on misconceptions can help diminish it.

2. **Positive Reinforcement**: Stand in front of a mirror and give yourself a pep talk before practicing a speech. Remind yourself that your audience is on your side, just as Sammy reminded me. This positive reinforcement will help build your confidence.

3. **Comfort Zone Expansion**: Challenge yourself to speak in front of progressively larger groups. Start with one or two people and gradually increase the audience size. This gradual exposure will help you

become more comfortable speaking in front of others.

4. **Feedback Collection**: After giving a speech, ask for feedback from your audience. Focus on constructive criticism and genuine praise. Use this feedback to improve your next speech. Understanding that feedback is a tool for growth rather than a judgment will help you embrace it.

5. **Support System**: Find a speaking partner or group where you can practice together and provide mutual support. Just as Sammy was by my side, having someone to encourage and give feedback can make a significant difference.

6. **Visualization with Detail**: Spend a few minutes each day visualizing yourself, giving a successful speech. Imagine every detail—the venue, the audience's faces, your gestures, and the positive feedback. This detailed visualization can enhance your confidence and reduce anxiety.

7. **Mistake Reframing**: Practice giving a short speech and intentionally making a small mistake. Then, calmly correct yourself and continue.

Mistake reframing will teach you that mistakes are not the end of the world and can be handled gracefully.

8. **Audience Connection**: Before your speech, take a few minutes to interact with your audience, if possible. Audience connection could be as simple as greeting a few people or conversing casually. Building a connection with your audience beforehand can make you feel more comfortable and supported.

By consistently practicing these exercises, you will build your confidence and develop the skills needed to become an effective and fearless public speaker. Remember, the journey to overcoming your fear of public speaking is a gradual process, but with dedication and effort, you can achieve your goals.

Chapter Four
FATHER KNOWS BEST: HOW MY DAD HELPED ME FIND MY VOICE

I was five years old and MISSING! My mother, heart pounding and frantic, raced around the house, calling my name. Silence echoed back. She dashed outside, asking the neighbors if they had seen me. No one had. The unthinkable thoughts crowded her mind: Had I been kidnapped? Had I run away from home at just five years old, tired of life already? The police were called, and a search party was quickly assembled. My mother tried to reach my father at work, but these were the days before cell phones, and immediate responses were a luxury.

Announcements blared over the radio, and television stations were contacted. The entire community was on high alert. After what felt like an eternity, my father was finally reached. Without a moment's hesitation, he raced home, determination etched into every line of his face. He burst through the front door, eyes scanning the room with laser focus, then turned left and headed straight down the hallway to my room.

With a calmness that belied the chaos, he approached my bed. Slowly, he knelt as if preparing to pray and reached his long arms underneath. Out from the shadows, he gently pulled a young, sleeping five-year-old Paul. Somehow, the heart of a father knew. He knew I loved playing with my cars under the bed and must have drifted off into a very long, peaceful nap. At that moment, all the fear and worry melted away, replaced by the overwhelming relief of a father's love and the miracle of a child found.

This story from my childhood is more than just a memory; it's a lesson in understanding the essence of who we are and how we communicate. My father's intuition, his ability to find me when no one else could, mirrors the journey each of us must take to find our unique voice. Just as my father knew where to look for me, we must learn where to look within ourselves to discover the voice that is distinctly ours.

Finding your voice as a speaker is akin to my father's search. It requires patience, intuition, and a deep understanding of oneself. You must navigate through the noise and distractions of life to find that place where your true voice resides. It's a journey of self-discovery, much like the journey I experienced as a child.

To be an effective speaker, you need to connect with your audience on a personal level. This connection begins with authenticity. Just as my father's love and intuition led him to find me, your authenticity will lead your audience to connect with you. They will sense your sincerity, just as I sensed my father's love.

As you embark on the journey of learning your voice, remember that it's not about perfection but about being genuine. It's about reaching into the depths of who you are and bringing that to the surface. Just like my father, who knew exactly where to find me, you need to know where to find your voice. It's there, waiting for you to uncover it, to nurture it, and to share it with the world.

This chapter will explore the path to finding your voice as a speaker. We will delve into practical steps and techniques to help you discover and refine your unique voice. We will look at ways to connect with your audience, speak confidently, and deliver resonant messages.

Always remember that the foundation of all these techniques is authenticity. Just as my father's genuine love led him to me, your genuine voice will lead you to your audience. Let's begin this journey together, discovering the powerful, authentic voice within you.

PRINCIPLES AND TECHNIQUES TO FINDING YOUR VOICE AS A SPEAKER

SELF-REFLECTION AND UNDERSTANDING:

Take time to reflect on your personal experiences, values, and beliefs. Understand what drives you and what stories have shaped your life. This self-awareness will serve as the foundation for your authentic voice. Ask yourself questions like, "What am I passionate about?" and "What experiences have deeply impacted me?" Journaling your thoughts can help you uncover more profound insights about yourself. This practice allows you to connect deeply with your own story, making your message more genuine and compelling.

EMBRACE VULNERABILITY:

In this generation, where everyone uses filters online, being authentic, and vulnerable is refreshing.

People connect and resonate with individuals who share their weaknesses. This is something Stan Lee, the legend behind Marvel Comics, understood profoundly. He knew that every Spiderman needed a nerdy Peter Parker. Peter's struggles and imperfections made Spiderman relatable and beloved. Your audience doesn't need a superhero; they need a real person to identify with. Share your challenges and how you've overcome them. Let your audience see the human side of you. This vulnerability fosters a deeper connection and trust.

PRACTICE ACTIVE LISTENING:

Listen to feedback from your audience and peers. Understand their needs, concerns, and interests. This will help you tailor your message and delivery to resonate more deeply with them. Engage with your audience during your talks. Ask questions, encourage participation, and be open to their input. This creates a dynamic and interactive environment. As Stephen R. Covey, author of

"The 7 Habits of Highly Effective People," said, "Most people do not listen with the intent to understand; they listen with the intent to reply." By truly listening, you demonstrate respect and value for your audience, making your communication more impactful.

DEVELOP YOUR UNIQUE STYLE:

Experiment with different speaking styles and techniques until you find what feels natural and comfortable for you. Your unique style will set you apart and make your presentations memorable. Watch recordings of your speeches to identify what works best and where you can improve. Incorporate elements of storytelling, humor, or emotion that align with your personality.

Embrace who you truly are. Some people will not like your style, and that's okay. Others will connect with you for the very same reasons others don't. There is a danger in trying to make everyone like you. When you try to please everyone, you can end up with nobody liking you, and worse, you won't like this mirage of yourself you are creating. Authenticity means being true to yourself, even if it means not being universally liked. Your distinct voice will attract those who resonate with your message and style.

CONTINUOUS LEARNING:

Study great speakers and learn from their techniques. Attend workshops, read books on public speaking, and continually seek to improve your skills. The more you learn, the more confident and versatile you will become. Join speaking clubs or groups where you can practice and receive constructive feedback. Surround yourself with other passionate speakers who can inspire and challenge you.

Learning is a lifelong journey, and every new piece of knowledge adds to the richness of your voice. Read books, including this one you're reading now, to expand your understanding and skills. Remember, as the saying goes, "The more you learn, the more you earn." Continuous learning not only enhances your speaking abilities but also opens up new opportunities for growth and success.

STORYTELLING:

Stories are a powerful tool for connecting with your audience. Share personal anecdotes, case studies, or historical examples that illustrate your points. Stories make your message relatable and memorable. Structure your stories with a clear beginning, middle, and end. Ensure they have a purpose and tie back to the main message of your speech. A well-told story can evoke emotions, create a lasting impression, and make complex ideas more accessible. Look how many stories I have already shared with you in this book. Hopefully, they are connecting with you and building a relationship between us. As author and speaker Les Brown said, "Never tell a story without a point and never make a point without a story." Stories are the bridges that connect our hearts and minds, making our messages come alive.

FOCUS ON YOUR AUDIENCE:

Shift your focus from yourself to your audience. Consider their perspectives, questions, and needs. When your primary goal is to serve and connect with your audience, your voice will naturally become more genuine and impactful. Conduct audience research before your speech to understand their demographics, interests, and pain points. This will help you tailor your content to their specific needs. The more you know about your audience, the better you can connect with them.

Make it your priority to serve and help the people you are speaking to. Your goal should be to add value to their lives and meet them where they are. A good practice is listening to other speakers at the event and observing what connects with the audience. You can learn a lot by watching videos of previous events and noting what resonates with the audience. This not only helps you tailor your message but also shows your respect and dedication to understanding and serving your audience. Zig Ziglar once said, "You can have everything in life you want if you will just help enough other people get what they want."

PRACTICE, PRACTICE, PRACTICE:

Consistent practice is key to finding and refining your voice. Rehearse your speeches, seek opportunities to speak in front of different audiences, and be open to constructive criticism. Record yourself practicing and review the footage to identify areas for improvement. Practice in front of friends or family members and ask for their honest feedback. Practice not only helps you refine your delivery but also builds your confidence.

I recently stumbled upon an old cassette recording of one of my speeches from over 25 years ago, and I was horrified to listen to it. The growth I have experienced since then is tremendous. Always have a hunger to grow. Embrace every opportunity to practice and learn, knowing that each step forward brings you closer to mastering your voice. This constant drive for improvement will keep you evolving as a speaker and ensure your message remains fresh and impactful.

AUTHENTICITY OVER PERFECTION:

Aim for authenticity rather than perfection. Authentic speakers are relatable and trustworthy, whereas striving for perfection can come across as robotic and disconnected. Embrace your imperfections and use them to your advantage. They make you human and relatable. Your audience will appreciate your honesty and openness. Remember, it's your genuine connection that leaves a lasting impact, not a flawless performance.

And let's talk about mistakes—because they will happen, and that's okay. Learn to embrace them, laugh at them, and grow from them. Imagine you're giving a speech and suddenly losing your train of thought. Instead of panicking, acknowledge it with humor. Say something like, "Well, there goes that thought! I guess even my brain needed a break." This not only makes you more relatable but also eases the tension in the room. Remember, it's these human moments that create a real connection with your audience.

I remember one of my earliest speaking engagements; I was nervous, and my lips were dry, so I took a quick sip of water from the glass by the podium. As I continued speaking, I accidentally burped into the microphone. It was only the second time I had ever spoken publicly! Instead of letting it derail me, I humorously acknowledged it, saying, "Well, I guess my nerves needed a voice, too!" The audience laughed, and it became a moment of connection. Remember, it's these human moments that create a real bond with your audience. As Bob Ross would say, "We don't make mistakes, just happy little accidents."

EMBODY YOUR MESSAGE:

Live out the messages you share. When your words align with your actions, your voice carries more weight and credibility. Be a role model for the values and principles you speak about. Your actions will reinforce your words and inspire your audience to follow your example. Authenticity in your daily life will enhance the authenticity of your message.

Finding your voice is a journey, not a destination. Just as my father's genuine love led him to find me, your genuine voice will lead you to your audience. Let's begin this journey together, discovering the powerful, authentic voice within you.

Finding your voice as a speaker is a deeply personal and ongoing journey. It's about embracing who you are, sharing your unique perspective, and connecting with others on a genuine level. You will uncover the authentic voice that resonates with your audience through self-reflection, vulnerability, active listening, and continuous learning.

Remember, it's not about being perfect. It's about being real. Embrace your imperfections and use them to your advantage. More than anything else, your authenticity will leave a lasting impact on your listeners. Just as my father's genuine love led him to find me, your genuine voice will lead you to your audience. Let's continue this journey together, discovering the powerful, authentic voice within you.

EXERCISES:

1: PERSONAL REFLECTION JOURNAL

Spend 15 minutes each day journaling about your personal experiences, values, and beliefs. Reflect on the following questions:

- What am I passionate about?
- What experiences have deeply impacted me?
- What stories from my life are worth sharing?

Review your entries weekly and identify common themes that define your unique perspective.

2: VULNERABILITY PRACTICE

Choose a personal story that involves a challenge or mistake you've made. Practice telling this story aloud, focusing on how you overcame the challenge. Share this story with a close friend or family member and ask for their feedback on how it made them feel. This practice will help you become more comfortable with vulnerability in your speaking.

3: ACTIVE LISTENING SESSIONS

Engage in conversations with friends, family, or colleagues with the sole intention of listening. Ask open-ended questions and focus on understanding their perspectives without interrupting. After the discussion, write down what you learned about their needs and concerns. Reflect on how you can incorporate this understanding into your speaking.

4: STYLE EXPLORATION

Record yourself giving a short speech in three different styles:

1. Storytelling with humor

2. Emotional and heartfelt

3. Informative and factual

Watch the recordings and note which style feels most natural and effective. Ask for feedback from others on which style resonated with them and why.

5: CONTINUOUS LEARNING PLAN

Create a learning plan for the next three months. Include books on public speaking, workshops, and online courses. Set specific goals, such as reading one book per month or attending two workshops. Keep track of your progress and reflect on how each learning experience enhances your speaking abilities.

6: EMBRACE MISTAKES

Set up a mock speaking session with friends or family. During the session, intentionally make a small mistake (like losing your place or mispronouncing a word). Practice acknowledging the mistake with humor and continuing your speech confidently. Reflect on how this exercise makes you feel and how it affects your connection with the audience.

> Engaging in these exercises will cultivate the self-awareness, authenticity, and confidence needed to find and refine your unique voice as a speaker. Embrace the journey, and let your genuine voice shine through.

HEY SPEAKPRENEUR!

I HOPE YOU ARE ENJOYING THIS BOOK AND FINDING IT VALUABLE. IF YOU'RE SERIOUS ABOUT TAKING YOUR SPEAKING SKILLS TO THE NEXT LEVEL, I HAVE SOMETHING INCREDIBLY EXCITING FOR YOU.

RIGHT NOW, AT SPEAKPRENEUR.COM, THERE'S AN EXCLUSIVE OPPORTUNITY WAITING JUST FOR YOU. THIS SPECIAL OFFER IS DESIGNED TO HELP YOU ELEVATE YOUR SPEAKING GAME, BUILD A POWERFUL PERSONAL BRAND, AND TURN YOUR TALENT INTO A LUCRATIVE AND EXCITING CAREER. BUT HURRY—THIS OFFER WON'T LAST FOREVER!

DON'T MISS OUT ON THE CHANCE TO TRANSFORM YOUR JOURNEY AND ACHIEVE THE SUCCESS YOU'VE ALWAYS DREAMED OF. VISIT SPEAKPRENEUR.COM NOW AND SEE WHAT AMAZING RESOURCES AND OPPORTUNITIES ARE WAITING FOR YOU. YOUR FUTURE AS A TOP-TIER SPEAKER STARTS HERE!

GO TO SPEAKPRENEUR.COM NOW!

Chapter Five
BIKERS, BOWTIES, AND BRIDGES: THE MAGIC OF A WELL-TOLD SPEECH

One of the most memorable compliments I've ever received came after a recent speech I delivered titled "Keep Dreaming." The audience was a sea of over 2,000 faces, but one stood out in particular. He was a rather large, burly man with tattoos covering his arms- a genuine biker-looking guy. Some might say he looked intimidating, but I could see a different story in his eyes as he approached me.

He extended his hand, his grip firm and sincere. "Whoa! That hit me hard!" he exclaimed. He went on to share that he had listened to all the other speakers and acknowledged their talent, but there was something different about my speech. "You took me on a journey," he said. "I was laughing one moment, nearly in tears the next." Then he uttered words that will forever be etched in my memory: "You changed my life."

I looked at him, this imposing figure who, by all outward appearances, seemed worlds apart from me. Here he was, a tough, rough-around-the-edges biker, and there I stood, a self-proclaimed nerd in a suit, bowtie, glasses, and shiny shoes. Yet, at that moment, it became clear that beneath the surface, we had more in common than I ever realized. We stood there, joking and chatting like old friends, barriers and preconceived notions melting away.

What happened here? In less than an hour, my words had transcended appearances and preconceived ideas. They had inspired, motivated, and, most importantly, deeply touched a soul. My words had brought light to his life, breaking down walls and bridging insurmountable gaps. Why did he feel a difference in my speech compared to others? First, I must acknowledge that my voice is a gift from God. I truly believe that He adds a special touch that I couldn't achieve alone.

I want to talk to you about that in this chapter—not just speaking to be heard but speaking to connect genuinely.

It's about making an impact, influencing, and changing lives.

How do you connect while speaking? Well, there isn't one simple answer to this question because each time you speak, you might connect with your audience in a different way. It's important to understand that how you connected last time may not be the same way you connect the next time.

You see, speaking is an art that requires an audience to help you get better. Think about it. A painter doesn't necessarily need an audience to improve his skills. A pianist can practice alone and still refine their craft. They can enhance in solitude or in a vacuum. But when it comes to speaking, you need an audience to determine what's working and what's not. There must be people to connect with and build bridges too.

So let me share with you my simple formula to remember to connect with your audience:

P.A.S.S.

P - PERSONALIZATION

Personalization means tailoring your speech to resonate with your specific audience. It's about stepping into their shoes and understanding their world—their hopes, dreams, fears, and frustrations. Dive deep into their interests, concerns, and expectations. Address them directly, weaving their stories, their language, and their experiences into your narrative. Make them feel like your speech is crafted just for them as if you're having a heartfelt conversation with each individual in the room. This creates a profound sense of relevance and engagement, turning a simple speech into a shared journey.

There is a certain danger in giving every audience member the same speech over and over. First, the speech will start to come across as stale and disconnected. It will lose its freshness and spontaneity, becoming a mechanical recitation rather than a living, breathing conversation. Secondly, the impact and influence you have will be significantly diminished. People will sense it. They will know if it's a canned performance, a rehearsed act rather than a genuine dialogue. A fake laugh, a recycled joke, or a speech that has been told a thousand times to everyone else will fall flat, failing to touch the hearts and minds of those listening.

Personalization is about bringing your audience into the heart of your message, making them feel seen, heard, and valued. It's about creating a unique experience that speaks directly to their needs and aspirations. When you personalize your speech, you're not just delivering words; you're forging connections, building bridges, and lighting a path that resonates deeply with those you speak to.

A - AUTHENTICITY

Authenticity involves being genuine and authentic to yourself. It's about standing in front of your audience, not as a performer reciting lines, but as a real person sharing real experiences. Speak from the heart, share your genuine thoughts and feelings, and let your unique personality shine through. When you are authentic, you invite your audience into your world, building a bridge of trust and understanding. You can't fake authenticity. Audiences connect more deeply with authentic and sincere speakers because they can sense the honesty and vulnerability behind your words.

Being yourself means embracing who you are, including your quirks, passions, and even your flaws. It's okay if your message is polarizing and doesn't appeal to everyone. Not everyone will agree with you, and that's perfectly fine. In fact, it's your unique perspective and personal truth that make your message powerful and memorable. When you speak authentically, you may not win over every person in the room, but you will deeply resonate with those who genuinely need to hear your message.

Remember, authenticity isn't about perfection. It's about being real. It's about sharing your journey—the triumphs and the struggles—and allowing your audience to see the human being behind the words. This genuine connection is what transforms a speech from a mere presentation into a meaningful conversation. So, let your guard down, speak your truth, and watch as your authenticity lights a spark in your audience, creating a lasting impact that goes far beyond the moment.

S - STORIES

Stories are powerful tools for connection. They transform abstract ideas into tangible experiences, making your message come alive. Share personal anecdotes, relatable experiences, or illustrative examples that bring your message to life. When you tell a story, you're not just conveying information; you're inviting your audience into your world, allowing them to walk in your shoes momentarily. Stories evoke emotions and help your audience see themselves in your narrative, fostering a stronger connection.

A well-told story can transport your listeners, taking them on a journey filled with ups and downs, triumphs and challenges. Through your stories, they can feel your joy, pain, struggles, and victories. This emotional connection is what makes your message memorable and impactful. Your audience will remember your stories long after they've forgotten the facts and figures.

In the next chapter, we'll delve deeper into the art of storytelling, exploring how to craft compelling narratives that captivate and inspire. But for now, remember that every story you share is a bridge to your audience's heart. Through stories, we touch souls, spark imaginations, and leave lasting imprints. So, embrace your stories, share them with passion and authenticity, and watch as they connect you with your audience in profound and meaningful ways.

S - SIMPLICITY

Simplicity is about keeping your message clear and straightforward. It involves avoiding jargon and complex language, instead using simple, impactful words and phrases that are easy for your audience to understand and remember. A simple, clear message is more likely to resonate and stick with your audience, leaving a lasting impression.

Research has shown that the most influential speeches are written at an 8th to 10th-grade readability level. This range ensures that your speech is accessible and engaging for a broad audience. When you simplify your language, you make your ideas more relatable and easier to grasp, no matter who is in your audience.

Adapting your style to fit the audience is crucial. Imagine speaking to a group of high school students about a complex scientific concept. You risk losing their attention and understanding if you use technical jargon and intricate explanations. However, if you break down the concept into simple, relatable terms, you capture their interest and enhance their comprehension.

A study published in the *Journal of Communication* found that messages tailored to an 8th-grade reading level were more comprehensible and engaging. This is why many of the greatest speeches, such as Martin Luther King Jr.'s "I Have a Dream" and John F. Kennedy's inaugural address, resonate so deeply. They employ clear, straightforward language that speaks directly to the heart and mind of the listener.

Consider the impact of simplicity in your speeches. You allow your core message to shine through when you strip away unnecessary complexity. This doesn't mean dumbing down your content; it's about refining your message to its most essential and powerful form. Simple language can convey profound ideas just as effectively, if not more so, than complex terminology.

Remember, the goal is to communicate, not to impress with fancy words. Your audience will appreciate a message that is easy to follow and digest. Focusing on clarity builds a stronger connection with your listeners, ensuring that your ideas are understood and remembered.

In essence, building bridges with your words is about creating a meaningful connection with your audience, transcending mere communication. Whether through personalization, authenticity, stories, or simplicity, each element of P.A.S.S. serves as a vital tool in crafting speeches that resonate profoundly and leave lasting impacts.

Personalization ensures that your speech is relevant and engaging, tailored to your audience's specific needs and interests. Authenticity invites your listeners into your world, allowing them to see the genuine person behind the words. Sharing stories transforms abstract concepts into relatable experiences, touching hearts and sparking imaginations. Simplicity keeps your message clear and accessible, ensuring that your ideas are understood and remembered.

Remember, every time you step onto the stage, you have the opportunity to bridge gaps and build connections that can inspire, motivate, and change lives. By embracing these principles, you not only enhance your ability to communicate effectively but also forge deeper connections with your audience, making your message truly unforgettable.

As we move forward, the next chapter will delve deeper into the art of storytelling, exploring how to craft compelling narratives that captivate and inspire. For now, embrace the power of P.A.S.S., and let your words build bridges that resonate with every listener. Each speech you deliver is a chance to touch souls and leave a lasting imprint, turning simple words into profound connections.

EXERCISES: BUILDING BRIDGES WITH YOUR WORDS

To help you apply the principles from this chapter and enhance your ability to connect with your audience, here are five unique exercises:

1. **Audience Persona Creation**: Create detailed personas for different segments of your audience. Imagine their age, profession, interests, and challenges. Write a short speech tailored to each persona, focusing on how you would address their specific needs and concerns. This will help you practice personalization and make your speeches more relevant and engaging.

2. **Authenticity Journal**: Keep a journal where you reflect on your speaking experiences. After each speech or practice session, write down what felt genuine and what didn't. Note moments when you felt most connected with your audience. A journal will help you identify and cultivate your authentic speaking style, ensuring that you remain true to yourself while addressing your audience.

3. **Story Inventory**: Compile a list of personal stories, anecdotes, and experiences that illustrate key points related to your core messages. Practice telling these stories in different ways to see which versions resonate most with various audiences. This exercise will help you develop a repertoire of stories ready for any speech, making your presentations more vivid and relatable.

4. **Simplify Your Message**: Take a complex topic you are passionate about and write a speech on it. Then, rewrite the speech with the goal of making it understandable to an 8th grader. Use tools like the Flesch-Kincaid readability test to check your work. Simplifying your message will help you practice simplifying complex ideas without losing their essence, making your message more accessible to a broader audience.

5. **Interactive Feedback Session**: Gather a small group of friends or colleagues and give a short speech. Afterward, ask them to write down the main points they remember and any specific parts that resonate with them. Discuss feedback and identify patterns. An interactive feedback session

will help you see what aspects of your speech are most effective and memorable, allowing you to refine your content and delivery for maximum impact.

> By consistently practicing these exercises, you will strengthen your ability to build bridges with your words, making your speeches more impactful and memorable. Remember, the journey to becoming a compelling speaker involves continuous learning and adaptation. Embrace these exercises as opportunities to grow and connect more deeply with your audience.

Chapter Six
THE BIRD TRICK THAT BACKFIRED: A STORYTELLING LESSON

Billy and Rod walked to school every day, and the highlight of their journey was stopping by the house of an older man who seemed to hold the wisdom of the ages. His presence was like a beacon of knowledge, his porch a sanctuary where stories flowed like a gentle stream. This older man had an uncanny knack for having the answer to any question posed to him. "Ask me anything, and I'll give you the answer," he would say with a twinkle in his eye.

Billy and Rod, in their youthful curiosity, found this both amusing and a bit annoying. No matter how tricky or obscure their questions, the older man always had a response. One day, as they trudged along the dusty path to school, Billy's frustration bubbled over. "We have to stump him," he said, kicking a pebble down the road. "Surely he can't have the answer to every question."

As they walked a little further, they saw a young bird on the ground, helplessly flapping its tiny wings. It had apparently fallen out of a nest perched high on the branch above. Billy's eyes lit up with a mischievous glint as an idea formed in his mind.

"Rod, I have an idea," he said, a sly smile creeping across his face.

"What? What?" Rod asked, intrigued.

"We are going to take this bird to the old man's house," Billy explained, his voice low and conspiratorial. "When we get there, I'm going to put the bird behind my back and ask him, 'Is the bird behind my back alive or dead?' If he says it's dead, I'll show him the bird, alive and well. But if he says it's alive, I'll squeeze the bird as tightly as possible, squeezing the very life out of it, and then show him it's dead. Either way, he'll be wrong. We've got him today."

Rod's eyes widened at the plan, a mixture of excitement and apprehension flickering across his face. They picked up the bird gently and set off towards the older man's house, their steps quickening with anticipation. The sun cast long shadows as they approached the familiar porch, the older man sitting there with his usual serene smile.

Billy hid the bird behind his back, his heart pounding with a mix of nerves and triumph. "Old man," he called out, trying to keep his voice steady, "Is the bird behind my back alive or dead?"

The older man looked at them, his eyes twinkling with the wisdom of many years. He momentarily paused, then said softly, "The choice is in your hands, my young friend. The choice is in your hands." Billy and Rod stood there, stunned into silence. The older man's words hung in the air, a gentle reminder of the power and responsibility they held. At that moment, they realized that wisdom wasn't about having all the answers but about understanding the choices they made. Their plan to outsmart the older man had been turned on its head, leaving them with a lesson they would carry for years to come.

This story about Billy and Rod, and the profound statement "the choice is in your hands," is one I've told more times than I can count. I've shared it in churches, at conferences with thousands of attendees, and in various other settings. Its ability to adapt and connect with almost any audience is truly remarkable.

Interestingly enough, I was about 11 or 12 years old the first time I heard this story. A speaker had visited our school, and we all sat in the gymnasium, listening intently. I don't remember much of what he said that day, but I do remember this story. Decades later, I find myself keeping this story alive because of its powerful impact on me. It's a testament to how a well-told story can transcend time and leave a lasting impression.

Stories are the lifeblood of communication. They are the threads that weave together our experiences, emotions, and wisdom into a tapestry that others can understand and relate to.

Here's why you should incorporate stories into your speeches:

EMOTIONAL CONNECTION

Stories evoke emotions. They make your audience feel joy, sadness, excitement, or empathy. This emotional connection helps to build a rapport with your audience, making your message more memorable and impactful. When you share a story, you invite your listeners into an emotional journey. For instance, sharing a personal story of overcoming adversity can elicit feelings of hope and inspiration. This emotional bond makes your audience more receptive to your message, as they feel a deeper connection to you and your experiences.

RELATABILITY

A well-told story can make complex ideas more relatable and understandable. It provides concrete examples that illustrate abstract concepts, helping your audience to grasp and retain your message more efficiently. Think about explaining a difficult scientific principle through a simple, everyday experience. Breaking down complex ideas into relatable scenarios makes it easier for your audience to understand and remember. Stories bridge the gap between theory and practice, turning abstract concepts into tangible insights.

ENGAGEMENT

Stories captivate attention. They break the monotony of facts and figures, drawing your audience into a narrative that keeps them engaged and interested. A good story is like a magnetic force that pulls listeners in, compelling them to pay attention. When you weave a narrative into your speech, you create a dynamic, immersive experience that holds your audience's focus. This engagement is crucial in maintaining their interest and ensuring your message is delivered effectively.

PERSUASION

Stories are powerful tools for persuasion. They can influence attitudes and behaviors by demonstrating the real-world impact of your ideas and by appealing to your audience's values and beliefs. As the saying goes, "facts tell, stories sell." For example, sharing a story about someone whose life was transformed by adopting a particular habit can be far more persuasive than simply listing the benefits of that habit. Stories provide a narrative context that helps your audience see the practical implications of your ideas, making them more likely to be convinced and motivated to act.

MEMORABILITY

People remember stories more than they remember data. A compelling story can stick in the minds of your audience long after your speech is over, ensuring that your message has a lasting impact. While statistics and facts are essential, they often fade from memory quickly.

In contrast, a well-crafted story with vivid details and emotional resonance can leave a lasting impression. Just like how I remember the story of Billy and Rod from my early childhood, stories embed your key messages in a way that facts alone cannot. By embedding your key messages within stories, you ensure that your audience retains and recalls your points more effectively.

HOW TO TELL GOOD STORIES

Now that you understand why stories are important, let's explore how to tell good stories that resonate with your audience. Crafting a compelling narrative is an art form that requires attention to detail and a keen understanding of your audience. Here are some key elements to consider when telling your story:

START WITH A GOOD HOOK

Begin your story with a compelling hook that grabs your audience's attention. A good hook could be a surprising fact, an intriguing question, or a vivid description. The goal is to draw your listeners in from the very beginning. Avoid starting your story with phrases like, "Let me tell you this story...". Instead, dive right into the action or the most intriguing part of your narrative. For example, starting with a line like, "Imagine finding a hidden treasure in your backyard," instantly piques curiosity and sets the stage for an engaging tale.

BUILD A NARRATIVE ARC

Structure your story with a clear beginning, middle, and end. Introduce the characters and setting, build up to a climax or turning point, and then resolve the story in a satisfying way. A good speech is often like watching a good movie. Think of your story as a journey with a destination and guide your audience through each step of the way. Next time you watch a movie, study the patterns they use while telling their story and see how you can apply similar techniques to your narrative.

USE VIVID DETAILS

Paint a vivid picture with your words. Use descriptive language to create strong mental images and to evoke the senses. Vivid details make your story more immersive and memorable. Describe your story colors, sounds, smells, and textures to transport your audience to the scene you're describing. For instance, instead of saying, "The garden was beautiful," describe the vibrant hues of the flowers, the fresh, earthy scent of the soil, and the serene feeling of being surrounded by nature. Good stories create feelings that resonate with your audience long after the story is told.

SHOW, DON'T TELL

Instead of simply telling your audience what happened, show them. Use dialogue, action, and sensory details to bring your story to life. Show, don't tell, makes your narrative more dynamic and engaging. For example, instead of saying, "John was angry," show his anger: "John slammed his fist on the table, his face turning red as he shouted." It can also be beneficial to incorporate memorable props into your speech. Props are fun and can help illustrate your points more vividly, making your story even more engaging and memorable.

INCORPORATE EMOTION

Don't be afraid to express emotions in your story. Emotions add depth and authenticity to your narrative, whether it's joy, sorrow, anger, or excitement. They help your audience connect with your story on a personal level. Share your feelings honestly, and your audience will feel them, too. For example, recounting a moment of personal triumph with a passionate voice can evoke empathy and inspiration in your listeners.

KEEP IT RELEVANT

Ensure that your story is relevant to your message and audience. It should illustrate or support the points you are making in your speech. A well-chosen story will enhance your message rather than distract from it. Tailor your narrative to the themes and lessons you want to convey, ensuring each element of your story aligns with your overall purpose.

PRACTICE, PRACTICE, PRACTICE

Like any other skill, storytelling improves with practice. Rehearse your stories until you can tell them naturally and confidently. Pay attention to your pacing, tone, and body language to enhance the delivery of your story. I'm not a fan of being dependent on using notes. You might start by using notes, but wean yourself off them as quickly as possible. Practice in front of a mirror, record yourself or share your story with friends and family to get feedback and refine your performance.

EXERCISES:

1. **Story Mapping**: Choose a personal story you want to share. Map out the narrative arc, identifying the beginning, middle, and end. Ensure that each part of the story flows logically into the next.

2. **Sensory Detail Drill**: Take a simple scene from your story and rewrite it with rich sensory details. Describe the sights, sounds, smells, tastes, and textures involved. Practice telling this detailed version to make it more vivid and engaging.

3. **Emotion Expression**: Pick a story with vital emotional elements. Practice telling it, focusing on conveying the emotions authentically through your voice, facial expressions, and body language.

4. **Audience Relevance Test**: Think of a story you want to use in your speech. Ask yourself how it relates to your main message and how it will resonate with your audience. Adjust the story to better align with your speech's purpose.

5. **Improv Participation**: Go to and participate in an improv show. This can really help you grow. Improv forces you to think on your feet, be spontaneous, and adapt quickly to changing situations, all of which are valuable skills for a storyteller. Plus, it's a fun way to build confidence and creativity in your storytelling.

> By consistently practicing these exercises, you'll enhance your storytelling abilities and become a more engaging and effective speaker. Remember, the art of storytelling is about making connections and leaving a lasting impression. Embrace your unique stories, refine your technique, and watch your speeches captivate and inspire your audience.

HEY SPEAKPRENEUR!

I HOPE YOU ARE ENJOYING THIS BOOK AND FINDING IT VALUABLE. IF YOU'RE SERIOUS ABOUT TAKING YOUR SPEAKING SKILLS TO THE NEXT LEVEL, I HAVE SOMETHING INCREDIBLY EXCITING FOR YOU.

RIGHT NOW, AT SPEAKPRENEUR.COM, THERE'S AN EXCLUSIVE OPPORTUNITY WAITING JUST FOR YOU. THIS SPECIAL OFFER IS DESIGNED TO HELP YOU ELEVATE YOUR SPEAKING GAME, BUILD A POWERFUL PERSONAL BRAND, AND TURN YOUR TALENT INTO A LUCRATIVE AND EXCITING CAREER. BUT HURRY—THIS OFFER WON'T LAST FOREVER!

DON'T MISS OUT ON THE CHANCE TO TRANSFORM YOUR JOURNEY AND ACHIEVE THE SUCCESS YOU'VE ALWAYS DREAMED OF. VISIT SPEAKPRENEUR.COM NOW AND SEE WHAT AMAZING RESOURCES AND OPPORTUNITIES ARE WAITING FOR YOU. YOUR FUTURE AS A TOP-TIER SPEAKER STARTS HERE!

GO TO SPEAKPRENEUR.COM NOW!

Chapter Seven
FROM BROKE TO BOOKED: PUBLIC SPEAKING, MY PASSPORT TO SUCCESS

Public speaking has transformed my life in ways I never imagined. It has taken me on a journey around the world, allowing me to experience some of the most beautiful places imaginable. I've had the privilege of visiting dazzling Dubai, charming cities in Europe, and vibrant destinations in South America. I've flown in private jets, met royalty, and had the red carpet rolled out for me. These extraordinary experiences were once beyond my wildest dreams, but they became my reality through the power of public speaking.

In addition to these incredible adventures, public speaking has connected me with some of the world's most well-known and influential people. From business moguls to cultural icons, I've had the opportunity to engage with individuals who are shaping the future. But perhaps the most astonishing transformation has been financial. I now have the ability to make more money in one hour than I used to make in an entire year.

This chapter is not just about my journey but about how to embark on a similar path. Whether you're passionate about inspiring others, sharing your expertise, or advocating for causes you believe in, public speaking offers a unique platform to make a difference while building a prosperous professional career. Let's explore how you can turn your passion for public speaking into a thriving career, just as I have.

REAL TANGIBLE WAYS TO MAKE MONEY AS A SPEAKER

1. PAID SPEAKER AT EVENTS

One of the most straightforward ways to earn money as a speaker is by getting paid to speak at events. According to a survey by the [Add Survey YEAR] National Speakers Association, the average speaking fee for a professional speaker is between $5,000 and $10,000 per event. Pay can vary significantly based on factors such as experience, niche, and audience size.

Being a paid speaker at events not only provides a significant income but also enhances your visibility and credibility. It allows you to showcase your expertise to a broad audience and build your reputation as an authority in your field.

2. WORKING WITH SPEAKING BUREAUS AND AGENCIES

Another effective way to secure speaking engagements is by working with speaking bureaus and agencies. These organizations act as intermediaries between speakers and event organizers, helping to match you with suitable opportunities. The benefits of working with speaking bureaus and agencies include:

- **Increased Exposure**: They have established networks and relationships with event planners and can help you reach a wider audience.

- **Negotiation Support**: They can handle negotiations on your behalf, ensuring you get the best possible fee for your services.

- **Administrative Assistance**: They take care of logistics, contracts, and other administrative tasks, allowing you to focus on delivering your speech.

3. HOSTING YOUR OWN EVENTS

I vividly remember one of the first events I organized with my good friend Chris. It was a modest gathering of about 50-60 people, but the experience was anything but modest. For two full days, we delivered solid content and connected with attendees in ways that are truly unique to in-person events. An indescribable magic happens when people gather in person—the handshake that turns into a bond, the palpable energy in the room, the collective excitement and fun. The atmosphere was electric. As we mingled with the crowd, we could feel the anticipation and enthusiasm in every conversation. The synergy of face-to-face interactions, the spontaneous laughter, and the shared moments of inspiration created an environment that simply can't be replicated online. Chris and I were not only thrilled with how the event unfolded but we were also astonished by the financial success. This seemingly small event generated over $200,000 for us. It was a clear testament to the power and profitability of a well-executed live event. To put it mildly, a well-done event can be incredibly lucrative. And this was just the beginning. Chris and I have since gone on to organize many more equally successful events together, refining our approach and expanding our reach each time. Every event has reinforced the incredible potential of live gatherings to create meaningful connections and substantial financial rewards.

Taking the initiative to host your own events, such as conferences, seminars, and masterminds, can be highly lucrative. This approach allows you to control the content, format, and audience, creating a tailored experience that delivers maximum value. There are several ways to monetize your events:

- **Ticket Sales**: Sell tickets to attendees, providing different pricing tiers based on the level of access or additional perks.

- **Sponsorships**: Partner with businesses or organizations that align with your message to sponsor your event in exchange for brand exposure.

- **Product or Service Sales**: Use the event as an opportunity to sell your programs, courses, books, or consulting services. An event can be an ideal platform to launch new offerings or upsell existing ones.

4. ONLINE SPEAKING OPPORTUNITIES

With the rise of digital platforms, online speaking opportunities have become a significant source of income for many speakers. These include:

- **Webinars**: Host live or pre-recorded webinars to your audience on specific topics of interest. Charge a fee for access or use them to promote your paid products and services.

- **Online Courses**: Create comprehensive online courses that provide in-depth training on your area of expertise. Platforms like Udemy, Teachable, and Coursera can easily reach a global audience.

- **Virtual Conferences and Summits**: Participate in or organize virtual conferences and summits. These events can attract large audiences and offer multiple monetization opportunities through ticket sales, sponsorships, and product launches.

- **Online Challenges**: Design and run online challenges that engage participants over a set period, providing value and leading to sales of related products or services.

EXERCISE SECTION

1. **Create a Roadmap to Earn $10,000 From Public Speaking**

    a. **Identify Your Niche:** Determine the specific area of expertise that sets you apart and resonates with your target audience.

    b. **Develop Your Personal Brand:** Build a professional website, create a compelling speaker profile, and establish a strong social media presence.

    c. **Create a Signature Talk:** Develop a high-impact presentation highlighting your unique insights and value.

    d. **Reach Out to Event Planners:** Network with event organizers, send proposals and leverage any existing contacts to secure speaking gigs.

    e. **Leverage Testimonials and Referrals:** Gather feedback from previous engagements and use positive testimonials to build credibility.

f. **Negotiate Fees:** Start with smaller, local events to build your portfolio, then gradually increase your speaking fees as you gain experience and recognition.

2. **Research Speaker Bureaus** Investigate various speaking bureaus and agencies. Understand how they operate, their requirements, and how they can help you secure speaking engagements. Reach out and consider forming a partnership to increase your exposure and opportunities. Learn from their experiences and strategies to refine your approach and enhance your visibility in the speaking circuit.

3. **Start Creating an Online Course Outline** Begin developing an outline for an online course based on your area of expertise. Consider the key topics you want to cover, the structure of each module, and the format of the content. Plan how you will engage your audience and deliver value through your course.

4. **Host a Webinar Series** Plan and host a series of webinars on topics that resonate with your audience. Decide on the format, frequency, and

pricing of the webinars. Promote the series through your network, social media, and email marketing. Use the webinars to showcase your expertise, engage with your audience, and drive sales of your products or services.

5. **Participate in Virtual Conferences** Identify and participate in virtual conferences and summits relevant to your field. Submit proposals to speak at these events, highlighting your unique insights and value to attendees. Prepare and deliver engaging presentations that leave a lasting impression—network with other speakers and attendees to build relationships and explore new opportunities for collaboration and growth.

HEY SPEAKPRENEUR!

I HOPE YOU ARE ENJOYING THIS BOOK AND FINDING IT VALUABLE. IF YOU'RE SERIOUS ABOUT TAKING YOUR SPEAKING SKILLS TO THE NEXT LEVEL, I HAVE SOMETHING INCREDIBLY EXCITING FOR YOU.

RIGHT NOW, AT SPEAKPRENEUR.COM, THERE'S AN EXCLUSIVE OPPORTUNITY WAITING JUST FOR YOU. THIS SPECIAL OFFER IS DESIGNED TO HELP YOU ELEVATE YOUR SPEAKING GAME, BUILD A POWERFUL PERSONAL BRAND, AND TURN YOUR TALENT INTO A LUCRATIVE AND EXCITING CAREER. BUT HURRY—THIS OFFER WON'T LAST FOREVER!

DON'T MISS OUT ON THE CHANCE TO TRANSFORM YOUR JOURNEY AND ACHIEVE THE SUCCESS YOU'VE ALWAYS DREAMED OF. VISIT SPEAKPRENEUR.COM NOW AND SEE WHAT AMAZING RESOURCES AND OPPORTUNITIES ARE WAITING FOR YOU. YOUR FUTURE AS A TOP-TIER SPEAKER STARTS HERE!

GO TO SPEAKPRENEUR.COM NOW!

Chapter Eight
THE SECRET SAUCE PEOPLE DON'T LIKE TO TALK ABOUT

I heard about a fascinating marketing experiment conducted by a company in a small community of about 25,000 people. They initiated a survey asking, "Who is the best real estate agent in the community?" The initial responses were scattered, with no clear winner emerging.

To address this, the marketing company launched a strategic campaign to promote their chosen real estate agent. They sent postcards and brochures to the entire community, but here's the twist: the name, photo, and information about this real estate agent were wholly fabricated. The agent was a fictional character, represented by a stock photo and invented details.

Incredibly, the survey was conducted again after just five weeks of this targeted promotion. This time, over 85% of the respondents identified the fictitious agent as the best real estate agent in the community.

This experiment powerfully illustrates that it's not always the best who wins but the best known. Perception, driven by strategic marketing and visibility, can significantly influence public opinion and recognition.

I'm not saying you shouldn't aim to be the best in your field—excellence should always be our goal. However, it's equally important not to be the best-kept secret in your industry. Balancing quality with visibility is crucial for achieving recognition and success. Attention is indeed the new currency. Without visibility, even the most talented professionals can go unnoticed. So, let's explore how you can transition from being unknown to becoming well-known.

BUILDING YOUR PERSONAL BRAND

One of the best investments you can make is an investment in yourself. If done properly, investing in your personal brand can have the highest ROI in anything you do.

I remember talking with a friend of mine who is an absolutely incredible speaker. He told me about a time he spoke at an event and left feeling slightly disappointed. He couldn't shake his disappointment despite speaking multiple sessions over two days and receiving accolades from attendees who said he was the best speaker at the event and that his words had changed their lives.

Why? Because he later found out that the concluding speaker of that event was paid ten times as much as he was. This speaker spoke for only 30-40 minutes, much less time than my friend. While he did a good job, it wasn't necessarily anything life-changing. So why did this speaker get paid ten times more? Because he was a famous online influencer. I won't disclose his name, but you've probably heard of him.

This experience taught us both a valuable lesson about the power of a personal brand. Having a strong personal brand opens doors for you. It leads to more opportunities and even higher pay. It's not always the best that wins; sometimes, it's the best-known.

Building your personal brand is about more than just being good at what you do. It's about ensuring people know who you are and what you stand for. Your personal brand should reflect your expertise, personality, and the unique value you bring to your audience.

A strong personal brand can set you apart in a crowded market and create opportunities for growth and success. It will change the game from you chasing clients to clients chasing you!

CREATE A PROFESSIONAL ONLINE PRESENCE

In today's digital age, a robust online presence is essential. Here's some tips on how to establish one:

DEVELOP A PROFESSIONAL WEBSITE

Your website is your digital business card. It should showcase your speaking topics, credentials, testimonials, and a portfolio of your work. Ensure its visually appealing, easy to navigate, and includes contact information. A well-designed website can make a lasting first impression and serve as a hub for all your professional activities. Don't go cheap on this and have someone's cousin's son who took a class in high school do your website. Hire a qualified, reputable company to do this for you. **Leverage Social Media Platforms**

Use social media to share your insights, engage with your audience, and build a following. Platforms like LinkedIn, X (formerly Twitter), Instagram, TikTok, and YouTube can be powerful tools for promoting your brand and connecting with potential clients.

I teach a simple formula for content creation called the I.C.E. method. This is a straightforward blueprint to help you grow, connect, and convert your online following into valuable leads and sales.

I - INTRODUCTION

Create content that continuously introduces you to your audience. Share who you are and what you do, including both exciting moments and everyday experiences. This is where you become real and authentic, allowing people to get to know you. Have fun with this.

C - CONTENT

Create content that provides value to your following. Share content that motivates, inspires, and helps them solve their problems. You can never go wrong by giving value. Consistently providing value will make your following more passionate and connected to you.

E - ENGAGE

Once you've introduced yourself and consistently provided value, move on to the next step: engagement. Show the product or service you are offering and encourage your audience to connect with you further. This might be done by clicking on a provided link or sending you a message in the DMs. People often say nobody ever reaches out to them; this could be because they are not intentionally displaying the services they offer.

Following the I.C.E. method, you can effectively use social media to build a solid personal brand, connect with your audience, and convert your following into leads and sales.

INVEST IN PUBLIC RELATIONS (PR)

People will often Google you before they contact you. You can control what message is being seen about you by investing in and working with a good PR team. Public Relations can help you manage your public image, get featured in reputable publications, and enhance your credibility. Here's how to leverage PR effectively:

PRESS RELEASES

Regularly distribute press releases about your latest speaking engagements, book launches, or other significant milestones. Press releases informs your audience and the media about your activities and achievements, ensuring you stay relevant and visible.

MEDIA FEATURES

Being featured in major publications can dramatically enhance your credibility and visibility. Strive to be featured in industry-relevant media outlets, podcasts, and blogs. Having your name associated with prestigious publications like Forbes, USA Today, Entrepreneur, or other major outlets relevant to your industry significantly boosts your credibility and positions you as a thought leader in your field. The ability to say you've been featured in these reputable sources can open doors and attract numerous opportunities.

LEVERAGE PODCASTS

Podcasts are a powerful platform for building your personal brand. They allow you to reach a dedicated and engaged audience. Here's how to make the most of this medium:

- **Guest Appearances**: Actively seek opportunities to guest on relevant podcasts. Share your expertise, insights, and stories. Guest appearances not only expand your reach but also introduce you to new audiences who might be interested in your services.

- **Start Your Own Podcast**: Consider starting your own podcast. Your own podcast can be a huge personal brand lifter. It allows you to control the narrative, share your knowledge, and engage with your audience more deeply. Your podcast can become a platform where you interview other experts, share your experiences, and provide valuable content regularly.

Investing in your personal brand is essential for standing out in the competitive world of public speaking. It's not enough to be excellent at what you do; you must also be known for it. You can improve your visibility and credibility by building a strong online presence, leveraging social media, and utilizing PR strategies. Remember, attention is the new currency. Make sure your expertise is well-publicized so you can attract the opportunities and recognition you deserve.

EXERCISE:

1. **Craft Your Bio**: Make your bio clear and concise on all your social media platforms. Use the formula: "I help [target audience] achieve [specific outcome or benefit] by [unique method or service]."

2. **Develop a Professional Website**: If you don't already have a website, invest in creating one. Ensure it showcases your speaking topics, credentials, testimonials, and a portfolio of your work.

3. **Leverage Social Media**: Use the I.C.E. method for content creation.

    a. **Introduction**: Create content that continuously introduces you to your audience. Share who you are and what you do, including both exciting moments and everyday experiences.

    b. **Content**: Provide valuable content that motivates, inspires, and helps your audience solve their problems.

c. **Engage**: Show the product or service you are offering and encourage your audience to connect with you further.

4. **Study Industry Leaders**: Study other speakers or thought leaders in your field. Observe their online presence, content strategies, and engagement techniques. Learn from their successes and adapt their methods to suit your brand and audience.

5. **Create a Speaker Reel**: Put together a speaker reel highlighting your best speaking moments. Aim for a 2-3 minute video that showcases your style, expertise, and audience engagement. A compelling reel can be a powerful tool for attracting speaking engagements and connecting with potential clients.

By following these exercises, you'll be well on your way to building a solid personal brand and turning your passion for public speaking into a successful career.

MY CONCLUDING THOUGHTS

As we reach the end of this journey together, I hope you feel empowered, inspired, and ready to take on the world as a true Speakpreneur. You have explored the depths of public speaking, discovered the secrets to captivating your audience, and learned how to transform your unique voice into a powerful tool for change.

Remember, the path of a Speakpreneur is a continuous journey of growth and learning. Every speech you give, every audience you engage with, and every story you tell is an opportunity to refine your craft and expand your influence. Embrace each experience with an open heart and a willingness to learn, for it is through these moments that you will truly shine.

You've seen how public speaking can open doors to extraordinary opportunities, from traveling the world and meeting influential people to creating a thriving and lucrative career. Your voice has the power to inspire, motivate, and transform lives. Never underestimate the impact you can make with your words.

As you step forward into the world, equipped with the knowledge and skills you've gained from this book, remember to stay true to yourself. Authenticity is your greatest asset. Let your genuine voice guide you, and let your passion for your message shine through in every speech you deliver.

The world is waiting to hear what you have to say. Your journey as a Speakpreneur is just beginning, and the possibilities are limitless. Go out there and make your mark. Inspire others, share your story, and use your voice to create positive change.

Thank you for joining me on this journey. I am excited to see where your path as a Speakpreneur will lead you. Remember, the power to shape the future is in your hands. Now, go, go, go! Share your voice, your story, and your message with the world!

I wish you much success!

Paul Getter

HEY SPEAKPRENEUR!

I HOPE YOU ENJOYED THIS BOOK AND FOUND IT VALUABLE. IF YOU'RE SERIOUS ABOUT TAKING YOUR SPEAKING SKILLS TO THE NEXT LEVEL, I HAVE SOMETHING INCREDIBLY EXCITING FOR YOU.

RIGHT NOW, AT SPEAKPRENEUR.COM, THERE'S AN EXCLUSIVE OPPORTUNITY WAITING JUST FOR YOU. THIS SPECIAL OFFER IS DESIGNED TO HELP YOU ELEVATE YOUR SPEAKING GAME, BUILD A POWERFUL PERSONAL BRAND, AND TURN YOUR TALENT INTO A LUCRATIVE AND EXCITING CAREER. BUT HURRY—THIS OFFER WON'T LAST FOREVER!

DON'T MISS OUT ON THE CHANCE TO TRANSFORM YOUR JOURNEY AND ACHIEVE THE SUCCESS YOU'VE ALWAYS DREAMED OF. VISIT SPEAKPRENEUR.COM NOW AND SEE WHAT AMAZING RESOURCES AND OPPORTUNITIES ARE WAITING FOR YOU. YOUR FUTURE AS A TOP-TIER SPEAKER STARTS HERE!

GO TO SPEAKPRENEUR.COM NOW!